Theater of Parts

Sundress Publications • Knoxville, TN

ISBN: 978-1-939675-33-0
Library of Congress: 2016933168
Published by Sundress Publications
www.sundresspublications.com

Editor: Erin Elizabeth Smith
Editorial Assistant: Jane Huffman
Special Thanks to: Graham Bonnington

Colophon: This book is set in Adobe Gurmukhi.

Cover Image & Design: T.A. Noonan

Book Design: Erin Elizabeth Smith

Theater of Parts

M. Mack

Acknowledgements

With gratitude to the journals and anthologies where the following poems previously appeared, sometimes in alternate versions:

Adrienne: A Poetry Journal of Queer Women: "Discovery Narrative: an act in five plays," "Traveling: an act," and "What Doesn't Need to Be"
APARTMENT Poetry Quarterly: "Ambulating," "Interlude: Milquetoast Wonders on Dissociation," "Interlude: Transformation narrative," "Sideshow: Milquetoast Recruits Brood II," and "Sideshow: Milquetoast Joins Brood II"
Bared: An Anthology of Writing on Breasts (Les Femmes Folles Books, 2016): "In Between Acts: a dramatic fantasy," "Interlude: The Tits Dance Their Mournful Dance," and "Interlude: What The Tits Remember"
Cream City Review, Genre Queer Folio: "Bottle-neck Fists: curtain warming"
Fence: "In Between Acts: a dramatic fantasy," "On Cellular Memory," and "The Poet and The Actor Discuss Cellular Memory"
Gargoyle: "What Toast?"
Hysteria (Lucky Bastard Press, 2016): "Not a Lack: an image"
Menacing Hedge: "Traveling Again"
Rogue Agent: A Journal of Embodied Poetics: "Image and Lack: a spectacle"
Wicked Alice: "Not This"

Several of the sequences in this manuscript have been collected in the chapbook *Traveling* (Hyacinth Girl Press, 2015). Thanks to *Cahoodaloodaling* for first reprinting "What Toast?" online.

Contents

All this wretched traveling.

Franz Kafka
The Metamorphosis

(Alcohol comes in wearing the disguise of a cockroach. It is blue.
It crawls silently up Buster Keaton's leg.)

from "Buster Keaton Rides Again: A Sequel"
Jack Spicer
After Lorca

Milquetoast, n.

a bland, timid, or ineffectual person easily dominated
from Caspar Milquetoast (Americanism of "milk toast"),
character in H.T. Webster's *The Timid Soul* comic strip, 1924 to
1931 and later, Milquetoast the cockroach, purple crossdressing
character in Berkeley Breathed's *Bloom County* and *Outland,*
1980 to 1995.

And now, this.

What Toast?

When Milquetoast became a cockroach, he lost his mustache. He tried fulfilling this lack of apparent gender with a penchant for what he and many others understood as crossdressing, in a wig and an ugly green dress, but this became an occasional activity: the Christmas special, big fights or fancy dinners with Opus the penguin.

When Milquetoast was a man with a name given and not received, he longed for the silent middle syllable to assert itself in conversation. When given the opportunity, he pronounced it as the Spanish *what* or the English *wuh?* When folks called for *milktoast* like a menu item, he asked quietly *What toast?* and then accepted the menu item.

When Milquetoast is dressed up, he likes the way he is treated as dainty, fragile. Opus wears Milquetoast on his arm as easily as he wears his briefs or his masculinity. Milquetoast likes the way the others look at him as vermin to be toyed with, hunted, caught. When Milquetoast is dressed for an evening out, The Poet is an asshat and refuses to change his pronouns, says he likes the gender for the wrong episodic reasons, though what does ze really know about Milquetoast.

Milquetoast became aware of the politics of sex when he began dressing up with the wig and the dress. *Crossdressing from what?* He heard the whispers around town. *How do you sex a cockroach?* They said these things into one another's ears. The Poet Human offered, *something about the wing length.* He twitched his antennae beneath the blond curls, stood straighter to emphasize his cleavage, expose his clavicle—did he have a clavicle?—as he passed them by, his wings—did he have wings?—uncomfortably exposed.

Milquetoast became aware of the politics of language around the time he became aware of the politics of sex. He was a cockroach for fuck's sake—he could not escape the terminology of sex, drugs, and rock & roll. He felt most conscious of his crotch when he wore the dress. He felt neutral when nude and purple, not-gendered. This was the source of mystery after all—how do you sex a cockroach how do you sex a cockroach how do you sex a cock—

—But that was his own question. Opus was a standard distant beloved best friend nemesis character. Opus was baffling. Milquetoast thrilled from imagining their wings brushing, from remembering his feet on Opus's shoulder like a Jiminy Cricket messiah figure, his curls glowing this close to the light.

The Poet in hir search for a new name that doesn't make hir shudder in gender discomfort considers *Milquetoast* because of hir stubborn fondness for the letter M, because of the transmogrification inherent in man to cockroach to cockroach in dress, in becoming the other, and another. Ze, too, would like to pronounce the *what* syllable.

This idea makes Milquetoast the cockroach shudder and bristle. The memory of Milquetoast the man has milktoast drippings in his chin gristle. Later, The Poet Milquetoast asks quietly, *what toast?* but is soon answering to *milktoast* and speaking the silent syllable hirself. Listening to this, Milquetoast the cockroach stomps an enormous high heel on the table and asks, *twat toast?* The Memory of Milquetoast the Man wipes his chin on his shirttail, refuses the menu item.

Traveling
an act

Scene

The streets are cobbled, and the boys wear newsie caps. I want to acquire one—a boy, or a newsie cap. The long sticks are curly, and they lie in a pile on the stones. Maybe they are for sale. Many of them are broken. The boys select sticks according to height.

I met two potential lovers on a micro-blogging platform, but they each live in separate dimensions which you can only travel between on flying bicycles pedaled with long sticks. They each look like the bully from that TV show or like my annoying neighbor who I am lonely enough to talk to or maybe even fuck. I get them confused with one another, bicycling between burger joints in different dimensions. In one dimension, there is danger. A shortage of sticks. Many newsboys traveling. In their haste, the boys start getting their bodies confused with the other boys' bodies. They find themselves suddenly pedaling another boy's bicycle with another boy's sticks held in another boy's hands. Nobody knows whose body belongs to whom. There is no longer any hope in me finding either of my potential lovers. They could be in anybody's body. No one is in my body. I select two sticks and ride home short and sexless.

Image and Lack
a spectacle

The Actor stands center-stage, buff and beardy. The Actor considers the audience.

The Actor: Observe this.

The Actor begins deconstructing The Actor's body, beginning with The Actor's torso. The Actor removes shirt after shirt, scratching each against The Actor's face. The Actor's beard falls off in clumps.

The Actor stands center-stage, buff and breasty. The Actor considers the gaze.

The Actor: Observe this.

The Actor raises two hands and pinches The Actor's nipples. The Actor twists. The Actor's nipples come loose in The Actor's hands. The Actor brings The Actor's hands together, then apart. The Actor rolls The Actor's nipples in The Actor's right palm like cuff links, or dice. The Actor drops The Actor's dice nipples to the stage floor. The Nipples scatter. The Nipples are still and contemplative.

The Actor extends The Actor's arms to The Actor's sides. The Actor bends The Actor's arms at the elbows, brings each hand in to grasp a nipple-less breast. The Actor's hands twist toward one another and then move away from The Actor's chest, each still gripping. The Actor drops The Actor's tits to the stage floor. The Tits recover themselves from the splat of impact. The Tits begin to dance a mournful dance with one another. The Tits exit.

The Actor's chest gapes but does not bleed. The holes look only like nothing. Maybe like eyes. The Actor meets The Audience's gaze. The Actor exits.

The Poet *(from off-stage):* My chest gawks but does not see.

Later

The Tits scurry across the stage, tittering to themselves and looking for the cuff-link nipples. The Tits are gelatinous and bloodless, bumbling along like fists.

Traveling

an act

Scene

The locker room walls are lined with metal baskets filled with white shoes. The baskets are the kind yuppies special order from vintage-look wholesalers to decorate their homes with. The shoes are the kind no one is nostalgic for.

There is a woman there who wants me to try on all of the shoes. I insist this is ridiculous. She says the shoes are for the gymnastics team, and since I am the gymnastics team, I must try on all of the gymnastics shoes. I insist that I am not the gymnastics team, that the gymnastics team left in a bus full of girls. She looks at me, puzzling whether I am a bus full of girls. I am undressed for the shower. I consider covering myself in shoes. We each look around at each of the shoes. After a time, she walks through the doorway. She turns left.

Interlude: The Tits Dance Their Mournful Dance

The Tits are alone on the stage. The spotlight, dressed in red gel, comes on and then re-focuses down to their scale. The Audience wishes for opera glasses and is also glad to not have them. The Tits wear ruffled sleeves like dresses. The Tits have perched The Nipples on their heads like tasseled hats. The Nipples are afraid of heights and are prone to motion sickness, but they say nothing. Everything is red.

The music would be good for Blues-ing but The Tits are dressed for a Tango and they have little patience for the sink, sink, step-step of performed intimacy. The Tits prefer the power of long strides.

The Tits move next to each other in lines, boring really, like a too-prolonged Charleston. Their feet would move mirrored and together if they had feet. As is, they scoot along the floor of the stage, the motion choppy and startling. The Tits circle each other widely, then bump into one another when they come back together. They repeat this. They slowly take their distance, spin in their slow circles, then collide, their ruffled nonsense concealing the shock of each impact.

The Audience murmurs that The Tits are well-suited for partner dancing. They complement each other in size.

Traveling
an act

Scene

There is something like a spa there. The doorway is too wide and cannot be closed. The room is built for luxurious aesthetics and oblivious bodies. There are six tubs, maybe. Maybe a water fixture facade on the wall. Sinks. A closet with shelves. No doors.

The bathtubs are collapsible, which makes them difficult for bathing. The facility is singular, with specific times set in which men or women can use it. I sneak in between time slots. When I am in the collapsible spa tub, struggling in the plastic liner, naked on the floor, a beefcake stands in the wide doorway on his way to the racquetball court, and there is no hope for modesty. He stares at my chest. When I slide down in the tub to intersect my gaze and his, his gaze does not break. I am accustomed to this kind of gaze. I am still thrashing in the impossible tub. He walks off with his strange body in tow, considering my strange body. The closet fills with what is imagined and spills over. The spaces between the tubs are filled. The remaining plastics begin collapsing.

Little Generals

(Milquetoast is dressed for an evening out. He teeters on his enormous high heels, searching the stage.)

Milquetoast: Opus?

(The Poet enters, with enormous pen and tablet.)

The Poet: Here is my opus.

Milquetoast: Don't make me a metaphor.

The Poet *(writes this down)*: What would you like instead?

(Milquetoast stands beside The Poet and begins calling again for Opus.)

Milquetoast: Opus? Opus?

The Poet: Here.

(The Poet lays hir tablet down beside Milquetoast. Milquetoast climbs astride, his enormous feet filling the enormous page. Meanwhile, The Actor enters the stage, strides to center, and stands behind Milquetoast.)

The Actor: I speak from behind a character.

Milquetoast *(craning his neck to stare back and up at The Actor)*: Don't make me a metaphor.

The Poet: I am a metaphor.

(Behind The Actor, behind Milquetoast, The Memory of Milquetoast the Man shimmers and slurps.)

The Memory of Milquetoast the Man *(noticing The Audience beginning to notice him)*: Don't make me a character.

(The Poet stares at The Memory of Milquetoast the Man. The Poet bends down to pull the tablet from beneath Milquetoast's enormous feet. As The Poet pulls the tablet, The Poet speaks.)

The Poet *(hir head as high as Milquetoast)*: I speak through a character.

(The force of The Poet's breath, combined with the pull of the tablet from beneath his feet, causes Milquetoast to stagger backward. The Poet stands straight and steps to where Milquetoast had stood.)

Milquetoast the Cockroach: I am a character, standing here. I was standing there.

The Poet Milquetoast: I am a metaphor—

The Actor: Standing before you.

(The Tits giggle and scurry across the stage. The Actor observes them, covers the scar holes with The Actor's hands. The Poet crosses hir arms across hir chest, shifts and stares.)

Traveling

an act

Scene

The room is full of double beds. The beds are covered in those awful hotel quilted tapestry spreads. There is a bed fitted to a window frame. The frame is obsessively, delightfully, exact. The curtains are also quilted tapestry. The patterns melt into one another in the exaggerated pleats.

I am with an old friend and an older friend and a lot of people we know. I think, maybe I'll share the window bed with my old friend, but then I am in a top bunk with my older friend and I don't know where we are. We are topless and touching and she is a fantastic lover. She tells me what to do to her nipples, what to do with her breasts. I find this patronizing and arousing. I have the terrible pleasure of pinching one nipple away from her body, placing it on the wooden bed frame's edge, and rolling the heel of my hand across it, producing a violent twist. She shows me how to get the same effect in my hands, palm against palm.

The curtain slides down across our skin. When she comes, I stifle my screams.

Black Stage Dialogue

The Actor: The body is a text.

The Poet: The tits are the headline.

The Tits titter past.

Discovery Narrative

an act in five plays

origin

My shirt removed. A naked sculpture. I am encased in surgical mesh, my armature showing, stripped down to this. I am asking you to puzzle over me. The parts of me that are attractively masculine when clothed, attractively feminine when nude, are grotesque in this moment. I am packed into myself. The most naked I can be. I want you to help me out of my binder. To know what this is.

practice eroticizing

The pilot is unwilling to understand pain. He asked me to dress up like a boy for him. When he stripped me, he grabbed my chest through the mesh and grunted. He peeled my binder over my head, then the compression layer worn beneath. And then he grabbed them, gripping. I shoved him off; he landed on the bed casually, casually gazing. I squeezed my breasts, coaxing circulation or pleasure. He insisted he could be gentle; he began again. I came in one particular moment of pain, clamped my teeth down on his shoulder; he moved my face away, chiding, "No pain." Bruises like his fingers for a week.

when I was not the other

I was other in a lesbian bar, but dancing. And then against the wall. Mouth on mouth. My fist gripping abdomen, finding the familiar friction of shirt against binder there. I gripped harder then. Kissed harder. Placed fist on my abdomen, my friction.

avoidance

I do not always bind when we are together. My body does not always bother me when we are together. I would like you to read my body with your fingertips, to glean information from my sounds. I imagine your hands upon me, cool and soft on my scars, my parts. Trace me, my rough-hewn assemblage resisting female form. Trace me. I will not be afraid.

encounter

I imagine my body under your body. You slip your hand shyly under my shirt like a teenager. Instead of cool skin, you find warm mesh; it slips firmly against. Friction under your naked hand. No spectacle.

Interlude: Transformation Narrative

(Milquetoast is on the stage. The Audience is unsure of what observables happen next.)

The Actor *(enters and approaches)*: Milktoast?

Milquetoast *(softly)*: What toast?

(The Tits bring a tray of milktoast and memory. Milquetoast and The Actor observe this, the way The Tits balance the tray and rumble along beneath it. The Tits deliver the tray to Milquetoast. The Actor observes this.)

Milquetoast *(He sighs and begins slurping. His mustache gleams with the mess of it.):* This toast.

(The Memory of Milquetoast the Man shrinks and shivers. Milquetoast the cockroach, nude, purple, and neutral, is the size of the spoon's head. Milquetoast quicks and quivers. Milquetoast observes the milktoast. The Actor observes Milquetoast. The Audience is still unsure what is observable.)

The Actor: Is this how it happened? Meekly, over a tray of milktoast?

Milquetoast *(straightens his tiny purple shoulders)*: I chose the wig. I selected the dress.

(The Audience pays attention to something else for a while.)

Not This

this is not an act

Recent winter. Femininity in the form of warm clothing and crocheted accessories. Snow in a pretty, nonthreatening way. An evening like some kind of sitcom.

When I meet up with a man I am not-dating in the snow, I am hyper-aware of what is not happening. We are holding hands, and no one is watching. We are walking down the sidewalk, and no one is following us. Until, in a moment I cannot believe, he pulls me to him amidst the crowd on the crowded sidewalk. I don't know what he's doing until he's kissing me. People step around us, and they are not angry. When I hear yelling, I break away and brace myself for violence. People are smiling and cheering. Another straight-appearing couple is clapping. I am thoroughly confused. Later, he kisses me at his train platform. I enjoy this until I remember the last time I kissed someone at this train platform. This time, no one gives a shit. I tell him our privilege is showing, and I walk up the stairs to my platform. No one follows me. When I sit down on the train, an apparent woman sits down next to me. I, too, an apparent woman.

The Poet Dreams of The Actor's Body

There is probably fog and charismatic lighting.

The Actor stands center-stage.

The Actor raises two hands and grasps The Actor's nipples. The Actor's nipples disengage in The Actor's hands. The Actor brings The Actor's hands together, then apart. The Actor rolls The Actor's cuff links. The Actor extends The Actor's arm and places the gadgets in a silk-lined drawer, shiny with robotics.

The Actor extends The Actor's arms to The Actor's sides. The Actor bends The Actor's arms at the elbows, brings each hand in to unlock a nippleless mass. The Actor's hands twist toward one another and then move away from The Actor's chest, each still gripping. The Actor places The Actor's tits in the silk-lined drawer. The Actor raises two gleaming disks from the drawer. The Actor installs subtle pectorals.

The Actor extends The Poet's arm and as The Poet moves to install the tiny washer nipples—

Later

The Poet lies awake, still gripping hir chest, staring at a drawer lined with spandex and mesh.

Not This

this that is not an act

An older spring. A collage. At a college. New job, new peers, same body.

I cannot easily forget the moments of a new job. A man in the front lobby hesitant to meet with me. "Obviously you only like to work with women," he says, looking me up and down. His hand on my thigh under the table during our appointment. Me hesitant to tell my superiors. My superiors hesitant to tell their superiors. Me silent after that. Or co-workers in the back room unwilling to understand me partnered but not-lesbian. "Have you been fooling us?" "Is she an experiment?" "An exception?" I remember myself in a queer theory class one year prior, giving a presentation on transgender-exposé episodes of talk shows. I imagine myself in the trickster archetype, Sally Jessy rooting up photographs from my past. Me, carving out a space for myself, inside myself. These same new peers excitedly describing success for "gay marriage."

Interlude: If The Poet and The Actor Were Lovers...

The Poet keeps hir tits strapped down, so feels no pleasure. The Poet is human and The Actor is ether. The Actor is either. The Poet can see memory through The Actor's scar holes. For the first time, The Poet wants to complete them. The Poet wonders if The Actor wonders about prosthetics. The Poet wonders if The Actor can wonder about anything The Poet doesn't wonder about. When The Poet reaches out a fingertip to trace the edge of the right scar hole, the flesh around it forms a vortex. The Poet draws hir finger back in time, just as The Actor's chest snaps together, tied up at the new nipple. The Tits titter past. The Actor gasps and begs for The Poet to do the other one. One hole, one pectoral. The Poet reaches out one shaking finger. As The Actor's flesh begins to swirl, The Poet lurches out of the bed, out of the room.

Not This

neither act nor action

A recurrence. Friendly appropriation: How to intellectualize experience for an academic audience.

When my friend wants to describe what the word queer means in a political context meaning something different from gay, she cites an internet cartoon. An inked drawing: two white men in front of a white picket fence. The caption: "We're just like you. Racist, classist, sexist." My friend cites this cartoon and says, "Queer means not *that.*" I take this punchline as my own. In trainings, I define queer as "not that," and then I proceed to define *that.* This works well until I think too much about implication, until I remember the reclaiming of the word through institutionalization, the assumed whiteness and actual privilege inherent in all of this. Nothing is good enough. I say as much. The university officials in the training nod.

Sideshow: Milquetoast Recruits Brood II

Milquetoast, discovering a self alone on the stage, decides to enact a few recent experiments with the before-and-after body for The Audience. Milquetoast leads a set of cicadas onto the stage. The Memory of Milquetoast the Man drools in a ringmaster's top hat, leans on a white-tipped cane downstage.

Milquetoast *(gestures to the specimens and addresses The Audience)*: I, too, have had a body, and then a different body.

The Memory of Milquetoast the Man: Imagine getting stuck in your new body like a pair of jeans stuck around your ankles, fish-flopping to the bed not an option.

The cicadas, hearing the world flop, *attempt back flips.*

Milquetoast: Imagine wearing a new body inside your old body. Your new body must emerge, right?

When Milquetoast begins to consider wings, the emergence of wings, he shifts uncomfortably in his trampy tuxedo coat. He is still unable to pinpoint the precise moment of transformation. He cannot show The Audience these little bodies becoming others.

The cicadas are squirming on their backs, unaccustomed to their new costumes. Some of them fly their clumsy flight across the stage.

Observing the possibility of wings, Milquetoast slowly realizes that he is the one on the circus stand. It is sized for a man or a larger animal, not suitable for the insect troupe he'd imagined. He hops deftly down, exits the stage.

The Memory of Milquetoast the Man has a broom, not a white-tipped cane. He sweeps the cicadas along the stage floor.

The Audience considers weight, considers that when Milquetoast the man changed shapes, he reduced in mass, became more mobile. Not bigger. Not less.

Black Stage Dialogue

The Actor calls after The Poet, and The Poet calls back.

The Actor: I am tired of the clean, bloodless postmodern body.

The Actor: The parts white and pristine.

The Poet: I'm not.

The Actor smooths the flesh of The Actor's chest, ignores The Actor's scar holes.

Not This

an act or an action

Another older spring. To publicly negotiate gender in a same-sex not-divorce.

My new friends are beginning to implement what I have taught them about the vocabulary of genderqueer and trans identity, about preferred pronouns. They observe her masculinity in their memory and accidentally support her in undercutting mine. When they ask how things are going, they omit pronouns, or they use a hesitant *ze* to refer to her. I smile. I state a simple, "She prefers feminine pronouns." What I want to do is yell, *She's a she!* What I want to do is admit, *She's a butch. She's outside of your frame of reference because she's outside of mine.*

The Poet Steps into the Role of The Actor then Conflates Public and Private Space

The Poet draws a bath, heats pots of water on the stove and then pours them, considers pouring the just-boiled liquid onto hirself, then remembers hir flesh. Ze pours the water into the tub, then begins to pour hirself.

The Poet steps into the water, sinks hir body down into it. Ze drapes a striped towel over hir stripped self so that ze can bask in hir body without seeing its stripes.

The towel is warm and heavy in the water. Its weight like restraint.

The Poet flicks water at the candle tips on the tub's ledge, creates a tiny scene of rain and fog. Ze imagines for a moment Milquetoast, toweled, antennae wet and squiggly. The image in an armchair, lounging. Tiny umbrella drink, too. Maybe a palm frond.

The Poet looks left, out over the audience, and holds up a hand.

The Poet: When my fingertips do not wrinkle in the water, I wonder if I have fingerprints at all.

When The Poet looks back to the bath, hir hand is The Actor's hand again. The fingerprints still smooth and firm.

The Actor: Go ahead. Inscribe them.

The Poet: I do not need your consent.

Not This

was this an act or an action

An older winter. Long day at a conference in a neighboring city. Impromptu dinner with this man I know.

I am on something like a date with a man who identifies as straight. I happen to be dressed as something like a man. When we walk close together down the city street, I hear shouting and I listen. We have been called fags. He is unaffected; he never felt called to listen. I guide us into a restaurant. The waiter exclusively talks to me. We have a nice meal.

Sideshow: Milquetoast Joins Brood II

Seeing an empty stage again, Milquetoast constructs a circus once more. He leads the cicadas onto the stage. He drags out bottle-caps this time, one for each. They climb up onto them. The effect is something like choir risers.

Milquetoast: Having constructed harnesses, I am much better prepared for strapping on—

The Tits titter past.

Milquetoast: for flight.

And with that, Milquetoast mounts. One giant insect atop another. (All is relative.) The Audience finds this curious, considers again the potential of wings on the back, the curious itch there.

When the cicada takes off, it crashes a few feet away under the weight of wings, the weight of pilot. Milquetoast stands, smooths his squiggled antennae, staggers away from the slime. The Memory of Milquetoast the Man wipes his chin from the wings—the stage wings—fearful the slime is his.

Milquetoast: There are millions of them. I never considered myself a predator.

Milquetoast exits. Cicadas exit opposite.

Black Stage Dialogue

The Actor: Will you allow me my body.

The Poet: Who will allow me my body.

Not This

enact or inaction

Recent winter. Traveling for a job. A room, two double beds. Three women and a not-woman. White linens. A desperate desire for sleep.

I share a hotel bed with a woman I'm attracted to. This is not for sex, but for economy. I am expected to behave straightly—chastely—not only as not interested in women but also as a woman—for this night. The thing about this woman's body is that it reminds me of my not-partner's body. When I get into the bed, she is already asleep. I am careful not only to not disturb her, but also to not touch her. I have been accused of hyper-sexuality before. Probably all of us have. I leave what I think is a one-foot trench in the center of the bed, but I often mis-judge the size of my body. I am not surprised, then, when I feel her against me. But I am surprised, violently, by the feel of her against me: the curve of her belly fitting into the curve of my back. The warm heat of this spreads to my entire length, like something that should be relaxed into; at this proximity, the gentle hairs of her belly pricking my skin. When I move away and away from her. When I start to slip from the edge of the bed. When I realize my skin is not exposed. When I know that I can't possibly be touching her, but that I can still feel the warmth and the prickling. Only then do I start to understand the weight of memory. I move back into the bed. I attempt to remind myself of what is real, and what is not real. And when I struggle to sleep, I dream of her—not of the straight woman I am bedded with but of the butch woman she reminds me of—and also—thank you for the also—of a man I love. In the dream, he genders me correctly.

Interlude: Backstage Urination Attempts

The Tits have separated. Each Tit acts as a doorstop, each holding open one door to the public restrooms. Tit 1 chose women. Tit 2 chose men. In haste and efforts to simultaneously avoid looking at The Tits, protect the scar holes from potential Tit mounting, and suppress a strong desire to piss, The Actor walks into the wall between the two doors, The Actor's elsewhere-turned head the point of contact. The Actor crumples to the floor. Milquetoast emerges from the door marked Women, drying his hands on the skirt of his dress. Eye to eye with Tit 1, he gives an awkward curtsy. One of The Nipples gives a jaunty jump on Tit 1's head in a hat-tipping gesture. The Tits, enjoying the interplay between their agency and The Actor's anxiety, scuttle past The Actor's body and reunite with one another. After their exit, Milquetoast is struck by an idea, albeit more gently than The Actor struck the wall. Milquetoast settles into the left scar hole, ready for a ride on The Actor's chest, once again perched like an ill-placed conscience. Milquetoast is ready to remember the world from this height. Milquetoast hopes The Actor will soon stand.

In Between Acts
a dramatic fantasy

Act 1.
We are in the kitchen cooking up desire
Act 1.
When you palm my chest it is the flat of my desire
Act 1.
When you palm my chest it swells with your desire

Act 2.
When you undress me you discover my armature
Act 2.
When you undress me there is no need for armature
Act 2.
When we undress there are two swollen things on my chest
but you ignore them you don't ignore them there is no need
for armature there is no need there is only need

Act 3.
We lay down together two flat chests together
Act 3.
We lie down together my breasts are in the way
Act 3.
We lie down together our chests are flat together
my breasts are in the way we push them toward
pleasure we pay them no meaning no measure
Act 3.
Our chests made flat together and we push them toward pleasure

Act 4.
If this is an act
Act 4.
If this is an act, I am not an actor

Act 4.

I am not an actor you do not accuse me
actress you do not assume your actor

Act 4.

This is an act where we do not act where my chest is flat
you pay no mind my breasts are in your hands this is an act
where these acts can occur and do they do act here we do act

Act 5.

When we act together our bodies do what we do they follow our cues
(the director waves signs and shouts)

Act 5.

When we act together we are not not actors we are active not

Act 5.

When we act together our bodies follow cues
We mine them for pleasure we play them

Black Stage Dialogue

The Actor and The Poet parody the erotic mirror.

The Actor: I am my body.

The Poet: You are my body.

The Actor: I am tired of my body being your body.

The Poet: I am tired of my body being your body.

Traveling Again

a reaction

Scene

The house my friend lives in is like my grandparents' house, or like the house I grew up in; it reeks of untraceable familiarity. It folds in on itself, on the people trying to trace it. The house is many places at once. The house is fine with this. Its visitors struggle.

My friend walks out of the house. Theirs is a solitary decision, but I start gathering my things. I, too, have wanted to stake a claim with absence. Leaving is not effortless. I look for my shoes, but I find instead a papasan chair beneath a heap of strange stuffed things, a frame creaking with weight. The heap breathes in deep, shaking breaths. So do I as I leave it. I trip on a pile of shoes that does not breathe. I find three wingtips, unable to tell which two are mine until I find the fourth.

The Actor Encounters The Poet When Stage Becomes Page

What if the self is a shell.

The Actor: If you're going to ask me to open up my chest like a birdcage.

The Poet: I used to consider her body my home. Then I considered that she had subsumed me into her body. When her parents moved to town her father gave her the wrought iron birdcage I had always hated. I never understood storing mail and keys in something so…something. She put it in the living room, behind the couch, with the heap of things that only looked packed and ready to leave. I considered myself inside the cage.

The Poet remembers The Actor.

The Poet: I don't have to ask. There are probably window panes across your scar holes. I'll look into your chest eyes and see what's in there.

The Poet turns to look at The Actor. The Actor submits. Milquetoast is inside the cage. He looks relaxed and lovely. But before The Poet can finish projecting this image, ze sees he's already there.

Milquetoast is sitting in the left scar hole. His legs crossed, feet languid over the edge. One high heel dangling from his toe. Leaning back on his elbows. Like a pin-up.

The Poet: Or—Oh. There you are.

Milquetoast fluffs his wig in a hat-tipping gesture.

The Tits titter and bounce at The Poet's feet. The Poet nods politely at them, gently disentangles hir feet from their proximity, walks toward Milquetoast.

The Poet looks and looks at Milquetoast, sees no birdcage.

Traveling Again

a reprise

Scene

Market. The street is cobbled. The buildings that line the walk appear constructed of riches, flaunting in this construction the currency of broken and unwanted things.

Shoppers don't always know how to let go. Some clench their pocket lint and gum wrappers in their fists, unwilling to trade up and in. Not everyone has learned to un-want. I find a wooden bin filled with textiles. A lump of sweaters. Many have belonged to me. I find an orange sweater is now turquoise. It is femme and fine. I sling it over the strap of my satchel. This belongs to me. Then a plaid flannel, large and geometric. It is just right. I sling it over the strap of my satchel. This belongs to me. I pay for the things that belong to me, with things that belong to me. I am still rich with forgetting.

Black Stage Dialogue

Observed murmuring.

Milquetoast (or maybe The Poet) questions.

The Poet (or maybe Milquetoast) answers.

The Audience: Maybe it's hard to know oneself alone.

Sideshow: Milquetoast Has Wings and Doesn't Know Why

Milquetoast walks onto the stage. Lacking fingernails for a tuxedo manicure, he's got little silk gloves on all of his little legs, even shoved gloved feet into his shoes. Milquetoast isn't wearing a leather mermaid dress, but wants to be. He's got extra wigs on, piled up, coiled high and hard. He wears his wings out like a cape behind him.

The Tits stand off to one side with The Nipples like little microphones. The lights are dressed in red gel again, and Milquetoast is backlit with the gore of it. Milquetoast shows off his best femme snarl. She moves her arms in dramatic gestures but makes no sound. The Tits make sure their silence is in the same key.

Bottle-neck Fists

curtain warming

THE POET *stands center-stage under one spotlight. As ze speaks, figures of varying size and transparency rustle about in the shadows of the stage.*

The house is the house I grew up in.

The casserole dishes become serpentine when we pack them. We wrap them in cloths. They clot like memory. This one that we're wrapping is the one he smashed, a wedding gift, nineteen years old. This other one, its replacement, fourteen years old. It reeks of obligation, addiction, and expense. This seeps into my skin when I handle it; its bright flowers call up the brown ones in pieces, call up the *how will we replace it.* Here, they are both here. They are both intact. They each have teeth.

We met the conventions of the house. We learned to fold towels in fat squares to fit the squat closet.

We are in the house, as if we never sold it. We are coming back to collect our things. The house is full of things we thought we had carried with us, but here they exist outside of time. But the cat is not here. Does death exist in dreamspace? My father is here, overgrown and wispy, flitting in and out. My father's belongings are not here. Death does not exist in dreamspace, and death exists in dreamspace.

My mother's dolls stack and unstack themselves in motion like stop-motion. We watch them. Their colors swirl together in their cupped painted wood.

The curtains that came alive at night are here as barren shelving, populated by a stuffed thing here or there. The furniture is unlikely and undisturbed. When I open the drawers, I find plush soccer balls and basketballs. I pick each one up and squeeze its surface, and the process goes like this: I think I can cast it aside, but then I spot its face—eyes and mouth agape, an experiment in representation—and I know it is mine, and I know it must stay.

The house had four bathrooms, and they were each completely a color. White, pink, blue, yellow. Even the toilets. Even the tiles. Even the tubs.

But we are traveling, aren't we? We are deciding what we can carry when this representation begins to resent us. When the hallways fold on paper hinges, the upper floors turn to crawlspace, to cavernous bowls. The pink bath opens to the kitchen. The colors swirl together.

There, the cherry pitter mounted. The teeth about to strike.

When the house begins to fall down around us, we have to hold balls of yarn to our mouths to breathe. It is my job to roll the yarn. The balls get messier as I go. Sometimes, I just clot the mass from inside the skein together, wrap it a few times, hand it off, and begin again. Sometimes, they are all connected. We walk along, attached by breath and string.

Traveling Again

a reaction

Scene

The kitchen island stretches and breaks as I walk around it, forming an archipelago that floats around the corners of the house. Its pieces are uniform in size and speed, like the lines drawn behind street pavers. When it comes to it, the threshold is lonely. The outside of the house is as expansive as the inside is implosive, but the house asks that you try to take in one thing at a time.

Some friends are making a movie in the familiar house. She wants me to be an extra. He wants me to run lines. She wants me to be every extra. These are the same friends whose likenesses we spot in the backgrounds of our favorite movies. I extract myself from props and costumes, waxed mustaches and false breasts. It has taken all this time to put my shoes on for the walk home. I am leaving the threshold just as my friend is coming back in. The space between us compromised, we walk to the car impossibly close: they behind and also beside; arms fold around one another's hips, as if we could just—. When I turn my face, I have to reach only minimally. When their lips meet my reach, everything is gone. It's as if I've forgotten, and of course I have.

Bottle-neck Fists

a scene which is hard to see

A MEDICAL PROFESSIONAL, *or maybe just a draft of the* **DSM5**, *stands stage right for the duration of the show.*

The stage is covered in clear bottles in brown paper with fists gripped around their necks. **THE POET** *stands center-stage, observing the bottles and counting them.* **THE AUDIENCE** *cannot see the bottles.*

THE POET: The garage looked like this once. We found the trashcan on the farm just off our property, beside the fence that lined his walking path to meetings. She had one of us drag the can to the garage; I counted the bottles. I wrote the number down somewhere. It was a lot of meetings' worth.

A man who is dead but maybe surely maybe alive walks onto the stage from stage left. **THE AUDIENCE** *cannot see* **THE DEAD MAN**. *Neither can* **THE POET**, *because ze doesn't remember what he looks like, except for his nose.* **THE NOSE** *directs* **THE DEAD MAN**, *who is carrying a clear bottle wrapped in brown paper in his fist.*

THE POET: This isn't true. I remember exactly what he looked like. Except he appears tiny in my memory, like a photograph.

A **TINY MEMORY MAN** *appears. He is the exact size of* **THE NOSE**. *The two regard one another.*

THE NOSE—*and therefore* **THE DEAD MAN**—*approaches* **THE POET**. *The shimmery structure of* **THE DEAD MAN** *holds out an arm, offers the bottle.*

THE POET *considers this, then accepts the bottle from* **THE DEAD MAN** *and takes a long drink.*

When THE POET *drops the bottle onto the stage with the rest, it does not break.* THE TINY MEMORY MAN *considers this.*

THE POET *considers the bottle. Maybe it is plastic. Ze cannot remember, but has long suspected they were not glass. Ze can probably remember the sound of a bottle colliding with the sound of a body. Ze does not remember any of the bottles breaking, no matter where they were hidden. Ze does remember Tupperware.*

THE NOSE *is center-stage with* THE POET. *Ze considers* THE NOSE *and then touches hir face.*

THE POET: If I had been determined a boy at birth. He joked about holding an auction. I always thought he said "adoption."

THE NOSE *stands to the left of* THE POET.

THE POET: They were all relieved I didn't get his nose. Now I wish I had it. Nobody has it. Not even my brothers, but nobody has commented on this.

THE NOSE *stands to the right of* THE POET.

THE POET: What would it have been like if his nose rolled out of the box instead of the toe tag? I hate the word "cremains."

THE NOSE *takes this as a cue, draws* THE DEAD MAN*'s not-body forward to the stage floor. There is not much of a splat.*

THE POET *points and continues*: I could wear that nose. After his death, she showed me a picture of the two of them in college. He had 70s hair and 70s glasses. She had 70s hair and Groucho Marx glasses. You couldn't tell the two of them apart at first. I could put that nose on, and it would be like that. But there would only be me, no comparison.

THE POET *steps forward and starts to stoop.* THE POET*'s toe makes contact with the hazy outline of* THE DEAD MAN. THE POET *does a* *barrel roll over the body, scattering bottles.* THE TINY MEMORY MAN *regards hir body, the positioning of the bottles.*

THE NOSE *rises.* THE DEAD MAN *raises an invisible hand and grabs* THE NOSE *as if with a handkerchief, adjusts it firmly on his face.* THE POET *watches* THE NOSE *exit, sees it surrounded by the invisible, mutable outline of* THE DEAD MAN. THE AUDIENCE *watches* THE POET, *sort of disinterested, but sort of trapped in their grotesque chairs.*

THE FISTS *start dragging their bottles around, gripping toward the wrist, pointer and middle finger marching in toy soldier parody, frequently flicking off what they're facing.*

THE AUDIENCE *hears clinking glass.* THE POET *does not.*

THE TINY MEMORY MAN *leaps and shouts.* THE TINY MEMORY MAN *does a barrel roll of his own, skids between the fingers of a fist, dives into the neck of a bottle. He does not emerge.*

Two of THE FISTS *join forces, and the bottle is off the stage before* THE POET *can even reach for it.* THE FISTS *clear the remaining bottles with their lurching pace, kicking the extra along between them.*

THE POET *lingers a moment, and* THE AUDIENCE *wonders why.*

Exeunt.

Traveling Again

a reprise

Scene

Cobbled street. Boys with copper kettles on their heads. Girls with fishing rods arranged in their hair. People with their heads nude. Here, too, the shopkeepers accept bits of broken things as currency. Here, the shoppers have their fists full, their pockets.

When we are walking down the cobbled street looking at strange machines in windows. When I still have my satchel with two or three sweaters slung over the strap. When I stop to consider a cow made of copper bells and clockwork. When our fingers are entwined and we can kiss but they can also drift ahead. When the press of the crowd. When the flannel slips from the strap. When I am too tired to turn back for. When the push of upward motion on the narrow steps. When I find I am climbing. When the sight of their head, ahead, yet the feel of them in my hand, the thrum woven in.

Bottle-neck Fists
a scene of seeing double

THE POET *stands stage left.* **THE ACTOR** *stands stage right, then steps to the right.* **THE ACTOR** *becomes two actors.* **The ACTOR** *stands stage right, next to* **THE ACTOR. THE ACTORS** *take on the motions as* **THE POET** *describes them.* **THE ACTOR** *plays the role of* **THE POET. THE ACTOR** *plays the part of the friend, then the brother. Remember, there are two actors. Remember,* **THE POET** *is stage left.*

THE POET*:* My friend often drops his left hand heavy on my right shoulder then laughs when I tense.

THE ACTORS *make this scene—*THE ACTOR *in chair,* **THE ACTOR** *behind and beside, with hand on shoulder.* **THE ACTOR** *tense,* **THE ACTOR** *laughing.* **THE ACTORS** *dance the motions as* **THE POET** *speaks.*

THE POET: The first wave of instinct is to tuck right shoulder away from palm, send right elbow into gut, follow through with left hook around the body. The energy it takes to suppress the first wave of instinct is total.

THE ACTORS *pause. That is,* **THE ACTORS** *freeze.* **The ACTOR***'s fist in* **THE ACTOR***'s gut.* **THE POET** *with hir eyes shut.*

THE ACTORS *reset the scene.* **THE ACTOR** *in chair,* **THE ACTOR** *with hand on shoulder. Again, the choreography unfolds as* **THE POET** *speaks it.*

THE POET: What is left is the second wave of instinct. I am still. I am trembling from stillness. The energy required for keeping my body in place does not allow for the small movement of ducking out from under his hand. I move my jaw in tiny movements of *please move please move.* I am weak and funny. I fear I will have to let the first wave of instinct take over in order to get him to understand I hold my trauma in my right shoulder.

THE MEDICAL PROFESSIONAL: The brain cannot tell the difference between past emotion and present emotion.

THE POET: Maybe If I swung, I could leap backward fast enough that I would punch only air. Would he still laugh.

There is only one **ACTOR. THE ACTOR** *is frozen, flung backwards, bent in the back, arched toward the audience, left fist carried through.*

THE POET: It reminds me of playing house with my brother.

THE ACTOR *looks around for the second* **ACTOR.**

THE MEDICAL PROFESSIONAL: The adult child of abuse is often in a hyper-aroused state, the nervous system constantly on high as they anticipate unknown danger.

THE POET: When we were cooking dinner or doing our chores, he would squeeze the back of my neck or pinch my shoulders from behind in order to make me squeeze my shoulders up like a turtle, so hard that it hurt his fingers, and we would both panic-laugh.

THE ACTOR *has snuck up on* **THE ACTOR** *to enact this.*

THE POET: When I stopped breathing, he would stop. It was like we were practicing. It was like we were keeping our skills up. Years later, we recognized this behavior for what it was. We discussed flashbacks. He apologized for triggering them. We did not understand. We have not recovered the memory of the root.

THE ACTOR *lowers* **THE ACTOR***'s shoulders.* **THE ACTOR** *disentangles* **THE ACTOR***'s fingers.* **THE ACTOR** *stands beside* **THE ACTOR** *and waits.*

THE POET: Once, my grandfather, in a moment of physical affection, cupped my right shoulder with his bent arthritic fingers. It hurt. All I could do was not hurt him. I had already identified the position of the cane, how I could kick it to intercept his prosthesis, how my body weight would balance when his fell, when my brother came and removed his hand from my shoulder, gestured for me to leave the room.

THE ACTOR *looks at* **THE ACTOR. THE ACTOR** *does not act out this scene.*

Lights Fade.

Traveling Again

a reaction

Scene

I told you: The threshold is lonely.

When our lips meet, the shapes are all wrong, and we sit with them, and we sit still. Our lips stretch into strange lines. I move my hooked top lip against theirs in a grasp, and then we are still again. We are connected only by our strange lips and by the thrum of proximity. The wanting moves my lips again. They moves theirs against them. We are intertwined at this single point of connection. I don't remember what it looks like as it breaks. Later, we are still thrumming. We are still walking to the car. The backs of our hands are flush together. We bend our fingers backwards to entwine them. There is pain. There is also thrumming. It is warm.

Bottle-neck Fists

The Actors attempt wholeness

Before the curtain call, **THE ACTORS** *take advantage of the abandoned stage.* **THE ACTOR** *positions* **THE ACTOR** *opposite* **THE ACTOR** *on the stage. Then* **THE ACTORS** *charge like bulls, trying to reunite* **THE ACTORS***' selves, falling apart on impact.*

THE ACTORS *stand, join hands, and speak together.* I am tired of feeling powerless.

From the wings (the stage wings), **THE POET** *considers* **THE POET**, *considers this.*

Traveling Again
a reprise

Scene

Outside of town, on a train for lost things. Everyone on the train wears a nude head, except the conductor. Every traveler is jealous of the conductor's hat.

When they and I are on a train. When we share a seat, entwined at the arms and at the fingers. When we are warm and laughing. When there are strange machines to observe in the fields outside the windows. When we are tourists to them, touching their tiny distances on the paned glass. The ceiling of the train opens and lost items drop through correctly sized openings. A parcel floats onto my lap; a name tag flutters and settles. I have some understanding of absence and return. I do not consider if they does. This belongs to me.

Interlude: Milquetoast Wonders on Dissociation

Today, Milquetoast wonders if he has skin. If he bleeds. He wants to cover all of himself. He doesn't want to see any purple, any nude. The questions are overwhelming. Milquetoast, the complex system; his limbs, the simple parts. His arm, his arm, his arm looks strange. So do the other three. Which ones are legs. What do his antennae think of the wig? Do they resent him this quiet? He slips into her coverings, slides her shoes onto his feet like he's proud of them. She wears this comfort like a shroud.

Bottle-neck Fists

Curtain call

THE MEDICAL PROFESSIONAL *is still off to stage right with a steno pad.* THE NOSE *stands center-stage, the mutable body of* THE DEAD MAN *sunk down into the stage like he's standing through a trap door.* THE TINY MEMORY MAN *stands to the right of* THE NOSE. THE ACTOR *stands to the right of* THE TINY MEMORY MAN. THE ACTOR *stands to the right of* THE ACTOR.

MILQUETOAST THE COCKROACH *saunters onto the stage and startles when he sees the line-up, when he sees the scale, when he sees two of* THE ACTOR. THE MEMORY OF MILQUETOAST THE MAN *shivers and slurps behind him.* ***MILQUETOASTs*** *exit, shuffling and muttering about cues and stage times.*

THE POET *sits to the left of* THE NOSE.

THE MEDICAL PROFESSIONAL: Observe this.

To the left of THE POET, *shivering, a shiny not-image like* THE DEAD MAN. THE POET'S CHILD-SELF. *She is tall and blonde, holding an enormous silver-blonde tabby cat, a silver-scruffed terrier at her side. She looks at* THE AUDIENCE. *No one else does.*

They all begin to bow. Some of them stand up and walk off the stage. Some of them stay folded in half. Some of them exist.

Curtain.

Black Stage Dialogue

The Actor: So, they'll say, this is how you got to be this way.

The Poet: And I'll say, it doesn't matter how I got to be this way.

The Poet: I'll say, engage with me, this way.

On Cellular Memory

The Poet uses The Actor as a medical model of the medical model. There are two Actors. The Actor acts as a body. The Actor acts as a screen before the body. The Audience observes quite a scene.

The Poet: This little brain in my gut.

Ze points to the torso through the torso screen. The little brains illuminated. The chest holes thinking.

What Doesn't Need to Be

What Comes Pouring Out

There is a party. A building made of concrete that spirals. The top two or three curves constitute a roof. The party qualifies as a roof party.

I am at this party, mostly trying to avoid a woman I once loved and once nearly was. I am also trying to avoid all others that know this. Meanwhile, I act as a gender mentor to a few young people. At this party, folks wear IDs around their necks with words and images describing their selves and preferences. I am helping these young folks build false documents. People call them falsies, though no one seems to have an original. People wonder why I am not the government agency in charge of hanging identity documents. People wonder if I am.

Ambulating

When the ambulance of memory and distance comes roaring toward, its sirens swinging, The Poet wants resources.

The Poet *(to Milquetoast on hir shoulder)*: Help me plug my ears so I don't hear the sirens singing toward us.

The Poet *(to The Actor by hir side)*: Teach me to remove my ears.

Milquetoast is on The Actor's shoulder. They stand far away. They don't have to refuse.

OR

The Actor *(the two Actors speak together amidst the wailing and the lights)*: It's not the ears. It's the eyes.

The Actor has ears and also eyes. So does The Actor. The scar holes prism the lights.

OR

The Actor: You never taught us to collaborate.

But Milquetoast is on The Actor's shoulder, hopping in small tight circles, flashing purple and red. This Ambulance exits.

OR

The Poet on the quiet stage with the approaching quiet.

Milquetoast realizes that in a half an inch of water, he would surely drown.

What Doesn't Need to Be

What Grips Like Not Wood

There is a storm. We should evacuate the huge spiraling concrete tower, but the curves cost a lot of money for the host to rent. Guilt keeps us all there, gluing us to one another. The storm is also shaped like a spiral, the inverse of the tower. When the two spirals meet, they lock into each other like the dovetail joins on the rocking horse in the basement. The storm has a lot to hold on to. When the storm starts moving back upwards, it stretches the building along with it. The concrete spiral changes shape, pulling up and away and toward. The partygoers go, too, sucked up into.

When the storm lets go, the building snaps back, the concrete spirals collapse onto themselves. The survivors begin to unfold them, to look for more. We find pieces of clothing, empty, without their people. The people in the towering buildings surrounding this one assume there are no survivors, don't come looking. It starts to get a little *Lord of the Flies* in there, over the one surviving toilet paper roll and the somehow functioning floorplan a few levels down from the concrete folded like fabric. I start to inventory the survivors. I am looking for the woman I loved once, who must have been at the party, and maybe she is here. She is not. My mentees are present, but their falsies have been sucked away.

We know how these storms carry. We know that there is a place up there like Oz or Kansas in the sky, and if we want to find more survivors, we must go there, to in the sky.

Interlude: When Milquetoast Scaled the Crepe Myrtle

The man Milquetoast loved lifted him into the tree, then arranged his legs and cane around the trunk to hold him up. Milquetoast allowed this. As Milquetoast straddled the thin stalky trunk of the tree, as The Poet observed him, Milquetoast considered his life. Considered a new construction of felt and thread. Remembered when he was a man collapsed into himself. When he lived inside The Poet's collapse.

Milquetoast wants to be large, to feel large. There, astride one slim trunk of a large tree, Milquetoast wanted to scale the tree down to his size, his scale. Milquetoast wants to stall, to be not stalled. Milquetoast wants the man or The Poet to pick him up again. To be in hands. To be small, in hands.

Image and Lack:
a reprise

The Actor stands center-stage, blushed and beardless. The Actor is clothed and buttoned up tight.

The Actor has invited the others to watch. The Actor has an act to practice.

The Actor stands very still.

The Audience hears the buzzing long after The Actor hears it.

The Poet stares, clutches collar against chin, thinking of the swell of sting.

The Actor cocks The Actor's head to the right. The Actor slowly raises one hand to The Actor's throat. The Actor unbuttons once at the collar. A single insect exits. The Actor unbuttons twice more. Two more buzzing insects exit. The Actor unbuttons twice more, then twice more, and when the shirt falls open at the final button, The Actor collapses into a pile of clothing on the stage floor, a cloud of bees.

The Audience watches them fly off in different directions, shifts uncomfortable in their seats.

The Memory of Milquetoast the Man brings a laundry cart from the wings (the stage wings). He shuffles the pile of clothing into the cart, scatters the lingering flights.

The Poet watches all of this from the orchestra stand, still fisting hir collar closed.

Milquetoast drapes a window open lower in the placket of The Poet's shirt. Milquetoast stays very quiet, and The Poet stays very still.

What Doesn't Need to Be

To Launch a Rescue Operation

When we finally plan for it, we pull the rubberized once-concrete folds down into the surviving building, strap ourselves between the folds, and use the once-upper floors (pulled down into the once-lower floors) as a gigantic, impractical slingshot.

This works, of course. We land in the beautiful other. We are welcomed. Up there in the sky, they've been product-testing progressive children's toys. The party is there. They are nude. We are nude; our slingshot went back to the down there with our clothing. We are prepared to act as inventory checkers, to place our number 32 stickers into garments and onto metal puzzles. When I spot her, she smiles that smile like we were each other's. The kind of recognition you look away from. The keepers of the up there say if we inventory sticker-placers want to take the product testers back down, there is only one way: we will all be ejected into the out there, all at once. We will need to use our collective body as a wide net, catching and then joining hands. When we have collected enough bodies from the ether of the out there, our collective body will gravitate to the back down. This is all or nothing. At first, our net will be not wide enough, but then, too quickly, too heavy to control.

The Poet and The Actor Discuss Cellular Memory

The Poet: I thought the other day about giving you my tits.

The Actor: You've never taught me to question.

The Poet: If I got them removed, if I gave them to you, would they disappear into your scar holes?

The Actor: I want to ask what the tits remember. Those.

The Tits titter past.

The Actor: And those.

The Poet: Teach me to tear my tits off. Teach me to mutilate, and then regenerate. Teach me to transmogrify.

The Actor: Why?

Milquetoast watches from the wings.

What Doesn't Need to Be

To Be a Body Within a Body

I catch her easily on the way into the out there. Colliding with her body feels. We have formed a collective body already. We extend to catch a few friends, a few mentees. We see, a few feet off, the woman my woman loves. The friends on that end are tired. I am filled with the specific dread that if we don't catch her, this woman and I will be joined again. The weight of this adds to our collective body. I shove my left arm, thinking about extracting my body from the collective. I've shoved the friends on the left to the left. We float down, to the left. The friends extend their arms in a chain. The woman joins our collective body, and we go down like a breath.

Interlude: What The Tits Remember

If The Tits are honest with one another, they remember the pleasure brought from The Nipples before they wore them like hats. Pressure, also. An ache of muscle maybe like memory. The ability to move freely, attached to a body, the restraint of being held firmly against one and its breath. Tit 1 remembers a tic, a head jerking toward or away from. Tit 2 thinks of a ring of impressions. Teeth. A shudder. A claim. The Tits think of the softness of skin, the dents made by efforts of construction.

Black Stage Dialogue

The Poet: Not because.

The Poet: And.

Interlude: Milquetoast Befriends The Child Because The Child Needs a Friend

This isn't true.

Milquetoast befriends The Child because Milquetoast needs a new pair of shoes. Milquetoast assumes, quite rightly, that The Child will have boxes and boxes of plastic hyper-femininity. Milquetoast assumes that all of this hyper-femininity will be in his size. Milquetoast is frustrated to learn that the femme shoes are better suited for his antennae. That Ken's shoes fit, but really don't excite him.

Milquetoast thinks of crying when The Child re-works the worn-out heels, cuts tiny fabric leg warmers into strips, tucks fabric into the once-leather upper, re-tacks the soles, re-forms each arch. When he hears The Memory of Milquetoast the Man start to slurp behind him, he gestures for him to leave, for him to distract the drooling cat.

When the clay dries, when she slips Milquetoast's old but new again shoes back onto her feet, The Child whispers: I know all about transformation.

Milquetoast wonders if next time, they can cut the hair from one of the doll's heads to form a new wig.

The Child wonders if next time, they can cut her hair off to fashion a new wig, or several. She wonders if she could install a lift into Ken's heel. She wonders who first made Milquetoast's tiny custom shoes. She wonders what her mother would think of this latest art project.

What Doesn't Need to Be

What Recovery, In What Was Not Wanted, Owns

We are back in this place. It seems it's ours now. A roof garden has grown from the party spoils. My woman who is not mine handcrafts overly organized stalls from the rubber not-roof, a marketplace for the neighbors down below. We live in tents made from the textiles of the stall sides, of the clothing not claimed. The tower neighbors nearby still have no interest. The not-spiral tower is for no one else now. We've earned the place, I guess, or the glue of it. I feel out of. I feel within. I wonder if she.

Not a Lack

an image

There are two Actors.

The Actor stands center-stage. The Actor is clothed.

The Actor enters the stage, leading The Poet by the hand. The Actor leads The Poet to an audience seat on the stage. After The Poet sits, The Actor lifts Milquetoast from the left scar hole, places Milquetoast on The Poet's right shoulder. The Actor moves to join The Actor.

The Actor begins removing shirt after shirt. The Actor observes. The Poet observes. Milquetoast observes.

The Actor, undressed, has begun unfolding The Actor's body. After a few major gestures, The Actor has labial skin wrapped around The Actor's shoulders like a throw blanket. The Actor begins folding The Actor inward. The Actor considers the cultural conflation of anatomical structures. The Actor considers biological invagination. Social imagination.

The Actor observes. There is a folding and a turning. The Actor's head and shoulders are visible. A wide arc of skin around them. Then something like a lack that is not a lack. Not phallic. Not sapphic. An archway like a vulva, leading to the internal.

The Actor observes. The Poet observes. Milquetoast observes. The Actor observes.

The Poet reaches out a hand for The Actor, and Milquetoast stomps an enormous high heel down on The Poet's right shoulder. The Poet drops hir hand, scrunches hir shoulder, then relaxes it.

Milquetoast's antennae are scrunched and squiggly. She smooths her skirt.

The Actor approaches The Actor. The Actor's scar holes are gleaming. As The Actor approaches, The Actor's archway gleams in the same fashion. The Actor looks back at The Poet in a heart-tipping gesture. The Actor steps into the archway. The Actor completes the folding, the unfolding.

There are no Actors.

The Poet sits and observes. Milquetoast settles in on hir shoulder.

The Audience looks for a smattering of blood on the stage floor.

End.

Notes

Brood II is the group of magicicada that emerges every seventeen years in the northeastern United States, including where I live in Virginia. Periodical cicadas spend most of their lives as nymphs isolated underground. After the nymphs synchronously dig tunnels to the surface in the millions, they enter the pupal stage and then shed their hard digging shell to reveal their winged adult form. Within a few weeks, the adults mate, lay eggs, and die off. When the eggs hatch, they tunnel deep underground.

The poem "Sideshow: Milquetoast Has Wings and Doesn't Know Why" owes thanks to Paloma Faith for covering the INXS song "Never Tear Us Apart" and for making the music video that so greatly inspires Milquetoast to be the highest femme.

The poem "Ambulating" is framed by references to Russel Edson's poem "On Memory and Distance" and John Prine's happy enchilada song, "That's the Way that the World Goes Round."

Much of the foundational work for *Theater of Parts* was done in 2011 and 2012, while I was an MFA student at George Mason University. I offer my gratitude to colleagues and mentors who helped to shape this work. Thanks to J.K. Daniels, Brian Fitzpatrick, Wade Fletcher, Jackie Kari, Erika Lin, Rachael Lussos, Siwar Masannat, Sarah Musick, Eric Pankey, Kate Partridge, and Meg Ronan. For supporting me over time, shaping my reading, and helping me find my voice, thanks to Susan Tichy, Sally Keith, Ric Chollar, Mel Nichols, and Jennifer Atkinson. Thanks, too, to my students for naming me Mack, and especially to Devon Packett who drew the sketch that helped inspire the Milquetoast plushie.

I thank especially Michael Verschelden, who discovered Milquetoast with me as we watched Buster Keaton films. In the Netflix description for *Go West* was the word: milquetoast. For many hours, we scoured the internet, constructing the e(n)tymology for the insect version of the little tramp. Thank you, MV, for your wonder, and for recognizing her importance.

In 2013, I read Joseph Bernstein's Buzzfeed review of the depression simulator videogame *Actual Sunlight.* In his review, Bernstein quotes a passage from *Darkness Visible* by William Styron. That passage changed the way I understood this Theater:

> A phenomenon that a number of people have noted while in deep depression is the sense of being accompanied by a second self—a wraithlike observer who, not sharing the dementia of his double, is able to watch with a dispassionate curiosity as his companion struggles against the oncoming disaster, or decides to embrace it. There is a theatrical quality about all this, and during the next several days, as I went about stolidly preparing for extinction, I couldn't shake off a sense of melodrama—a melodrama in which I, the victim-to-be of self-murder, was both the solitary actor and lone member of the audience.

This work of the impossible body is impossible theater, a term coined by Caridad Svich in her collection of Federico García Lorca's drama. I owe much to the work of Lorca, Jack Spicer, Samuel Beckett, CA Conrad, and Gertrude Stein. Thanks to Kazim Ali, Anne Carson, Meg Day, Joy Ladin, Trace Peterson, TC Tolbert, Sonya Vatomsky, Ronaldo Wilson, and many others writing now, for exploding my understanding of what is possible.

Thank you to Erin Elizabeth Smith for believing in this work and to the staff and editorial board at Sundress Publications for all they have done to welcome me and my little theater. Thank you to T.A. Noonan for the incredible cover design, and to the Dramatist Play Service for providing the inspiration. Thank you to my writing group.

Thank you Bethany Dettwyler, Deedraye Halliston, Page Hodges, Bea Wallace Felter, Ruth Foley, Lucy Hochstein, Alyse Knorr, Ben Masters, Cherie Seise, Nicole Tong, Elise Wolf, and Sarah Ann Winn. Thanks to Bea, Beth, and Page for calling me home.

And finally, gratitude for Brian Picone, who left the world better.

About the Author

M. Mack is a genderqueer poet, editor, and fiber artist in Virginia. Ze is also the author of the chapbooks *Mine* (Big Lucks Books, 2016), *Traveling* (Hyacinth Girl Press, 2015) and *Imaginary Kansas* (dancing girl press, 2015). Mack is a founding co-editor of Gazing Grain Press and an assistant editor for *Cider Press Review*.

Other Sundress Titles

Every Love Story is an Apocalypse Story
Donna Vorryer
$14

Ha Ha Ha Thump
Amorak Huey
$14

major characters in minor films
Kristy Bowen
$14

Hallelujah for the Ghosties
Melanie Jordan
$14

When I Wake It Will Be Forever
Virginia Smith Rice
$14

A House of Many Windows
Donna Vorreyer
$14

The Old Cities
Marcel Brouwers
$14

Like a Fish
Daniel Crocker
$14.99

What Will Keep Us Alive
Kristin LaTour
$14

Stationed Near the Gateway
Margaret Bashaar
$14

Confluence
Sandra Marchetti
$14

Fortress
Kristina Marie Darling
$14

The Lost Animals
David Cazden
$14

The Hardship Post
Jehanne Dubrow
$14

One Perfect Bird
Letitia Trent
$14

The Bone Folders
T.A. Noonan
$14.99

CPSIA information can be obtained at www.ICGtesting.com
Printed in the USA
LVOW07s0301110316

478718LV00002B/20/P